5/15

The Countries

Lebanon

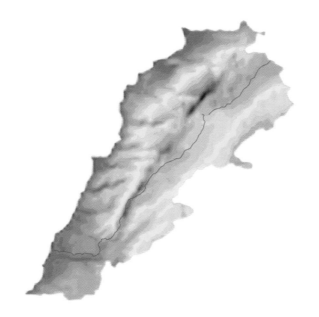

Kate A. Conley
ABDO Publishing Company

visit us at
www.abdopub.com

Published by ABDO Publishing Company, 4940 Viking Drive, Edina, Minnesota 55435.
Copyright © 2004 by Abdo Consulting Group, Inc. International copyrights reserved in all countries. No part of this book may be reproduced in any form without written permission from the publisher.

Printed in the United States.

Photo Credits: Corbis pp. 5, 9, 14, 17, 19, 20, 21, 22, 24, 27, 29, 30, 31, 33, 35, 37;
   Getty Images pp. 11, 25

Editors: Stephanie Hedlund, Kristianne E. Vieregger
Art Direction & Maps: Neil Klinepier

Library of Congress Cataloging-in-Publication Data

Conley, Kate A., 1977-
   Lebanon / Kate A. Conley.
      p. cm. -- (The countries)
   Includes index.
   Contents: Marhaba! -- Fast facts -- Timeline -- Lebanon's legacy -- Coasts, peaks, & valleys -- Plants & animals -- The Lebanese -- Building a new economy -- Cities to treasure -- From here to there -- Governing Lebanon -- Celebrating in Lebanon -- Sports & leisure.
   ISBN 1-59197-292-2
   1. Lebanon--Juvenile literature. [1. Lebanon.] I. Title. II. Series.

DS80.C663 2003
956.92--dc21
                                                                        2003044313

Contents

Marhaba!

Hello from Lebanon! Lebanon is a nation in the Middle East. It is home to some of the world's most ancient **cultures**. It is also home to some of the most beautiful beaches, mountains, and valleys in the world.

Life in Lebanon has not always been easy. Since ancient times, Lebanon has been conquered by many different groups. Each group has added to Lebanon's **unique** culture.

Today, Lebanon is recovering from a long **civil war**. The war greatly damaged the country. With peace restored, however, the Lebanese people are looking forward to a bright future.

Marhaba *from Lebanon!*

Fast Facts

BEIRUT

OFFICIAL NAME: Lebanese Republic (Al Jumhuriyah al Lubnaniyah)
CAPITAL: Beirut

LAND
- Area: 4,015 square miles (10,399 sq km)
- Mountain Ranges: Lebanon Mountains, Anti-Lebanon Mountains
- Highest Point: Qurnat as-Sawda 10,131 feet (3,088 m)
- Major River: Litani River

PEOPLE
- Population: 3,677,780 (2002 est.)
- Major Cities: Beirut, Tripoli, Byblos, Sidon, Tyre
- Languages: Arabic (official), French, English, Armenian
- Religions: Islam, Christianity, Druze, Judaism

GOVERNMENT
- Form: Republic
- Head of State: President
- Head of Government: Prime minister
- Legislature: National Assembly
- Nationhood: November 22, 1943

ECONOMY
- Agricultural Products: Citrus fruits, grapes, tomatoes, apples, potatoes, olives, tobacco; sheep, goats
- Manufactured Products: Cement, furniture, paper, detergents, cosmetics, pharmaceuticals, batteries, clothing, processed foods
- Mining Products: Iron ore, lignite, sand, lime
- Money: Lebanese lira (1 lira = 100 piastres)

Lebanon's flag

Lebanese paper money

Timeline

3000 B.C.	The Phoenicians arrive in Lebanon and later establish important cities
A.D. 300s	Christianity arrives in Lebanon
600s	Islam spreads to Lebanon
1000s	Druze faith arrives in Lebanon
1516	Lebanon becomes part of the Ottoman Empire; this empire rules Lebanon for about 400 years
1943	Lebanon becomes an independent nation
1975-1991	Civil war
2000	Israeli army withdraws from Lebanon

Lebanon's Legacy

Lebanon is an ancient land. It is home to some of the world's oldest human settlements. Some of Lebanon's early settlers were the Phoenicians (fih-NEE-shuhnz).

The Phoenicians arrived in Lebanon around 3000 B.C. They were excellent sailors and traders. They built mighty cities such as Tyre (TIRE), Sidon (SIDE-uhn), Beirut (bay-ROOT), and Byblos (BIH-bluhs).

Over time, the Phoenicians were conquered by different groups. The conquerors included the Egyptians, Assyrians, Babylonians, Persians, and Greeks. Later, the Roman Empire ruled Lebanon.

New religions soon spread to Lebanon. Christianity gained followers in the A.D. 300s. Arabs brought Islam to Lebanon in the 600s. In the 1000s, the Druze (DROOZ) faith spread across the country.

With so many religions in such a small area, people often fought for power. Then in 1516, Lebanon was conquered by the Ottoman Empire. This **Muslim** empire ruled Lebanon for about 400 years.

A wall of a Roman amphitheater in Byblos

After World War I, the Ottoman Empire collapsed. So, the **League of Nations** gave France control of Lebanon. France helped the country build a new government. Then in 1943, Lebanon became an independent nation.

The Lebanese worked to create a united country. However, the nation's many religious groups made this difficult. Over time, tensions grew. In 1975, a **civil war** broke out between Lebanon's Christians and **Muslims**.

The civil war lasted 16 years. During that time, thousands of Lebanese died. Peace was finally restored in 1991. Afterward, the Lebanese began rebuilding their cities and government.

The country still faced problems after the war. Israel's military occupied southern Lebanon. Fighting erupted between the Israeli army and Lebanon's **Hezbollah**. In 2000, the Israeli army agreed to leave Lebanon.

Rebuilding Lebanon has been a slow struggle after years of destruction during the civil war.

Today, the Lebanese are looking toward a brighter future. They strive to unite Lebanon's many different groups. Such work will undoubtedly strengthen this ancient, spirited nation.

Lebanon's Land

Lebanon is one of the world's smallest countries. In fact, the entire nation is about the size of the state of Connecticut. Despite its small size, Lebanon's land has many different features.

In the west, Lebanon borders the Mediterranean (meh-duh-tuh-RAY-nee-uhn) Sea. The coast is home to Lebanon's largest cities. Most of the coastal land is flat. It includes rocky beaches and sand dunes.

East of the coast, the land rises to form the Lebanon Mountains. They stretch nearly the entire length of the country. The highest peaks are covered with snow most of the year.

The Lebanon Mountains drop sharply in the east, forming the Bekáa (beh-KAH) Valley. The valley's land is fertile, so it is a major farming area. Farmers there grow grapes for wine. They also grow vegetables and grains.

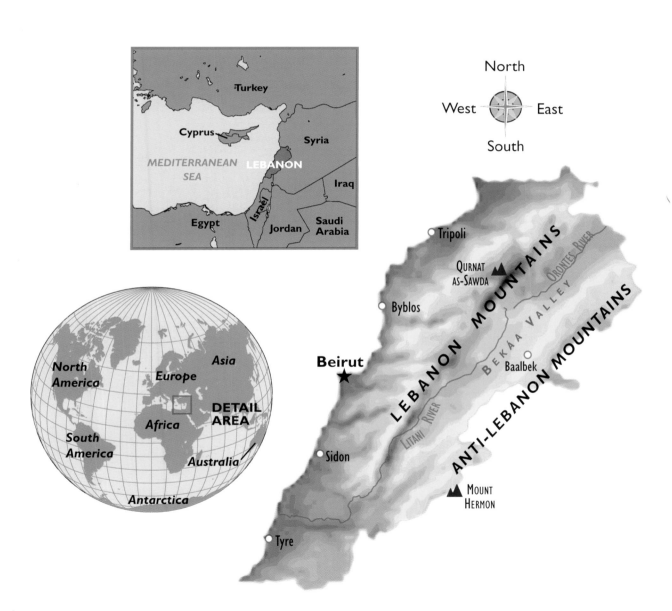

North

West East

South

Turkey

Cyprus

Syria

MEDITERRANEAN SEA

LEBANON

Israel

Iraq

Egypt

Jordan

Saudi Arabia

North America

Asia

Europe

Africa

DETAIL AREA

South America

Australia

Antarctica

Tripoli

Qurnat As-Sawda

Byblos

Beirut

Baalbek

Sidon

Tyre

LEBANON MOUNTAINS

ANTI-LEBANON MOUNTAINS

BEKAA VALLEY

ORONTES RIVER

LITANI RIVER

Mount Hermon

Farther east, the Bekáa Valley gives way to the Anti-Lebanon Mountains. Their highest peak is Mount Hermon. This peak has been considered a holy place for thousands of years.

Lebanon's major river is called the Litani (lih-TAH-nee). It is the only river in Lebanon that flows all year. The Litani begins in the Bekáa Valley and flows south. Later, it turns west and empties into the Mediterranean Sea.

The climate in Lebanon is mild. Along the coast, summers are hot and dry. Winters are cool and rainy. In the mountains, snowy winters and cool summers are common. The Bekáa Valley is cold and windy in the winter and hot and dry in the summer.

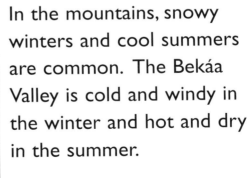

The Anti-Lebanon Mountains as seen from the Litani Dam

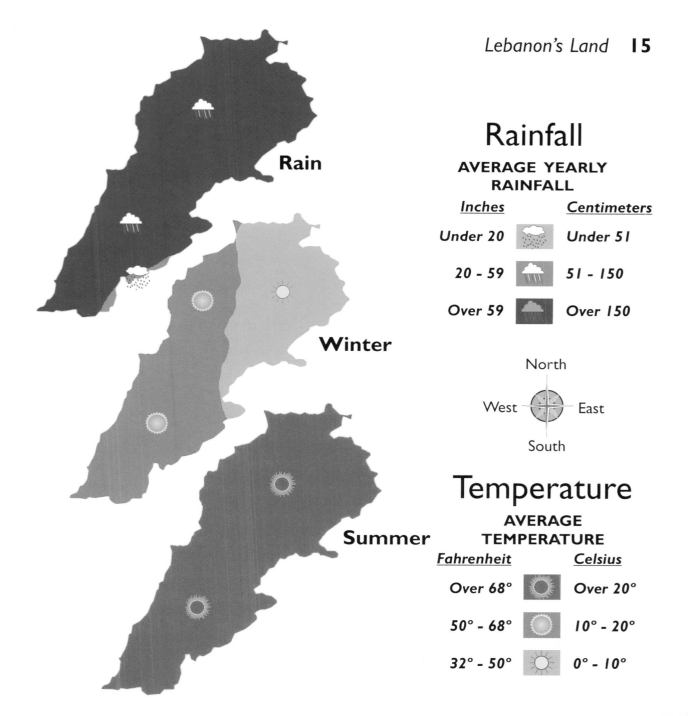

Rain

Winter

Summer

Rainfall

AVERAGE YEARLY RAINFALL

Inches		*Centimeters*
Under 20		*Under 51*
20 - 59		*51 - 150*
Over 59		*Over 150*

North

West — East

South

Temperature

AVERAGE TEMPERATURE

Fahrenheit		*Celsius*
Over 68°		*Over 20°*
50° - 68°		*10° - 20°*
32° - 50°		*0° - 10°*

Plants & Animals

The cedar tree is Lebanon's most famous plant. In ancient times, the country had vast cedar forests. Over the years, people cut down the trees and sold the wood. Today, cedar forests only grow on a few mountaintops.

Lebanon is home to many other kinds of plants, too. Oaks, pines, junipers, and cypresses grow there. In the spring, wildflowers grow on the mountains. Along the coast, fruit trees and palms are common.

Lebanon is also home to many animals, especially birds. They often stop in Lebanon during their migrations between Africa and Europe or Asia. These birds include storks, buzzards, and eagles.

Hunting is a popular sport in Lebanon. As a result, the country has few large animals. Many of those that remain are found in **reserves**. The Chouf Cedar Reserve is home to wolves, boars, wildcats, and foxes.

The Lebanese are proud of their cedar trees and want to save them from further damage. This helicopter is spraying the trees to protect them from insects.

The Lebanese

Lebanese people are a mix of several different groups. The main groups are the Phoenicians, the Greeks, and the Arabs. The country's largest **minority** group is from Armenia.

In Lebanon, the official language is Arabic. French and English are also commonly spoken. In fact, most Lebanese people can speak all three languages!

Lebanon's major religions are Islam and Christianity. Each of these religions is broken down into **sects**. The Shiites (SHEE-ites) are Lebanon's largest **Muslim** sect. The Maronites are Lebanon's largest Christian sect.

Besides Islam and Christianity, other religions are also practiced in Lebanon. The Druze faith is important to many Lebanese. In addition, some people who live in Lebanon are Jewish.

Opposite page: Children at school in Lebanon do many of the same activities American students do.

Families are very important in Lebanese society. People often stay in close contact with their relatives. Family events, such as weddings and funerals, are often large affairs.

Lebanese families live in different kinds of homes. In large cities, people often live in apartment buildings. In rural areas, Lebanese people often live in houses.

In general, Lebanese people wear clothing similar to that worn in the United States. In **Muslim** areas, the clothing is often more modest. Some Muslim women choose to wear a head-to-toe covering called a chador.

Lebanese students head home after a day of classes.

In Lebanon, people have many foods to choose from. A typical meal starts with *mezze*. *Mezze* includes dips or cheeses. The main course is usually mutton or fish. A popular dessert is baklava (bah-kluh-VAH). It is a pastry filled with nuts and covered with syrup.

Not all girls wear head coverings or chadors, but many schools do require uniforms.

Lebanon's national dish is called kibbe (KIH-bee). It is a kneaded mixture of lamb and wheat. Sometimes kibbe is served raw. Other times it is fried or made into a pie.

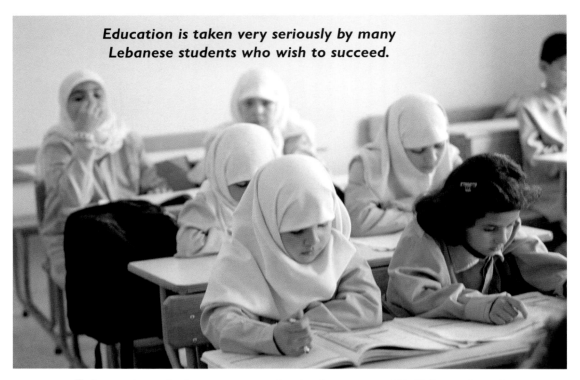
Education is taken very seriously by many Lebanese students who wish to succeed.

Education is important in Lebanon. Children begin attending school at age six. In school, they study subjects such as Arabic, English, French, science, social studies, and art.

After school, students enjoy many activities. Some students take part in scouting. It is a popular activity, so each school has its own scouting group. Other after-school activities include playing video games or sports.

Tabbouleh

Tabbouleh is a traditional Lebanese salad made with wheat and parsley.

- 3/4 cup bulgur wheat
- 2 large bunches parsley, finely chopped
- 2 tomatoes, finely chopped
- 1/2 bunch green onions, finely chopped

- 1/4 cup olive oil
- 1/4 cup lemon juice
- 1/4 cup mint, chopped
- Salt and pepper to taste

Soak the wheat according to the directions on the package. Combine the wheat, parsley, tomatoes, onions, and mint. Toss these ingredients. Then add the olive oil and lemon juice. Add salt and pepper to taste. Toss the salad and chill before serving.

AN IMPORTANT NOTE TO THE CHEF: Always have an adult help with the preparation and cooking of food. Never use kitchen utensils or appliances without adult permission and supervision.

English	Arabic
Hello	Marhaba (mahr-HAH-buh)
Please	Min fadlak (MIHN FUHD-luhk)
Thank you	Shukran (SHOOK-rahn)
Yes	Aiwa (AI-wuh)
No	La (LAH)

LANGUAGE

Building a New Economy

For many years, Lebanon was a center of trade. The nation had a strong **economy**. However, this prosperity ended during the 16 years of **civil war**. Today, Lebanon's people are rebuilding their economy.

Since the civil war ended, travelers have enjoyed visiting Lebanon's mountains, coast, and ancient ruins. So, tourism has become a growing part of the economy. Tourism creates jobs in hotels, restaurants, and shops.

Farming is also a major part of Lebanon's economy. A mild climate

Many people help rebuild Lebanon by donating money. These people are gathering to tour Beaufort Castle the day before an international donors conference.

and plenty of water allow farmers to grow everything from **citrus** fruits to vegetables. Two of Lebanon's major crops are grapes and potatoes.

Manufacturing is also part of the Lebanese **economy**. Factories make goods such as cement, furniture, paper, and other products. Some of the goods are sold in Lebanon and some are exported to other nations.

New buildings are being built all over the country. This helps improve Lebanon's economy by providing jobs.

Cities to Treasure

About 4 million people live in Lebanon. Most people live in cities along the coast. These cities are filled with ancient treasures and colorful histories.

Beirut is Lebanon's capital. It is located on two hills. The hills jut into the Mediterranean Sea. The city's location near the sea makes it an important port.

Beirut is also the largest city in Lebanon. About half of Lebanon's people live there. In fact, people have settled in Beirut for thousands of years.

Until the **civil war**, Beirut was a center of **culture** and business in the Middle East. However, the civil war heavily damaged the capital. Today, new businesses are replacing many of the bombed-out buildings.

Just north of Beirut is the ancient city of Byblos. It is one of the world's oldest cities to be lived in continually. People have lived in Byblos for 7,000 years!

This newly constructed section of the Arab Highway connects Beirut with the Bekáa Valley and other Arab nations. It will improve Lebanon's transportation, trade, and communication.

In ancient times, Byblos was a major shipping center. Goods such as cedarwood and **papyrus** were shipped through its harbor. Today, Byblos is still a busy city. It is often called by its modern name, Jubayl.

North of Byblos is Lebanon's second-largest city, Tripoli. It is a major port, a center of business, and a popular vacation spot. It is also known for its soap. Some locals even claim soap was invented in Tripoli!

Sidon is another major city in Lebanon. It is located south of Beirut. Sidon was a powerful Phoenician city. It was famous for its glassware and purple dyes. Today, the city is a center of trade for nearby farmers.

South of Sidon is Tyre. For years, it served as the Phoenicians' principal city. Over time, many other groups seized this valuable port. Today, ruins from these groups can be seen throughout Tyre.

Opposite page: Roman remains often lie right next to modern cities, such as these ruins in the city of Tyre.

From Here to There

Most of the transportation in Lebanon is by car. This works well due to the nation's small size. A person can drive from one end of Lebanon to the other in about three hours.

Lebanon has a large system of roads. One major road runs along the coast. Another runs through the Bekáa Valley. The coast and valley are connected by a series of mountain passes.

The country's location along the Mediterranean Sea provides the nation with many ports. Lebanon's main port is in Beirut. It transports most of the nation's passengers and cargo.

There are numerous ways to travel in Lebanon, even on boats!

Lebanon has only one airport, the Beirut International Airport. It is a new building that was constructed shortly after the **civil war** ended. It's quickly regaining its place as one of the Middle East's busiest airports.

Some farmers travel to and from their fields on donkeys.

Governing Lebanon

Lebanon is a **republic**. It is divided into six governorates, which are similar to states. They are ruled by governors who represent the central government. Local leaders govern Lebanon's towns and villages.

The National Assembly makes Lebanon's laws. The Lebanese elect 128 assembly members. They are divided between Christian and **Muslim sects**.

Assembly members select Lebanon's president. He or she serves as the head of state. In turn, the president appoints the **prime minister**. He or she is the head of Lebanon's government. The prime minister chooses the government's **cabinet**.

Opposite page: Lebanese leaders attend a festival celebrating Israel's withdrawal from Lebanon.

Religion is a factor in who controls Lebanon's government. By custom, the president is a Maronite Christian. The **prime minister** is a Sunni (SU-nee) **Muslim**. The speaker of the assembly is a Shiite Muslim. Leaders from all three **sects** work together to govern Lebanon.

Celebrating in Lebanon

Many of the holidays in Lebanon are based on religion. An important **Muslim** holiday occurs after the month of **Ramadan**. During that month, Muslims **fast** between sunrise and sunset. When the month is over, they celebrate with a feast called Eid al-Fitr.

Christmas is an important Christian holiday. On Christmas Eve, families attend church services and children receive gifts from Papa Noël. On Christmas Day, people spend time visiting family and friends.

Lebanese people also celebrate holidays that are not religious. On New Year's Eve, people often have parties in their homes. At the stroke of midnight, everyone crowds into the street to celebrate.

Lebanon also has many festivals. One of the largest is in Baalbek (BAY-uhl-behk). The Baalbek Festival draws musicians and dancers to the city. There, they perform in front of Baalbek's ancient Roman temples.

These Shiite Muslims celebrate Ashura, which is a holy day in the first month of the Islamic year.

Lebanese Culture

For centuries, people in Lebanon have made **cultural** contributions to the world. For example, the Phoenicians invented an alphabet with 22 letters. It is the base of today's English alphabet.

Another part of Lebanon's culture is dance. The national dance is called *dabke*. It is a five-step dance in which people hold hands. *Dabke* is usually performed at weddings and other social events.

Music is another important aspect of Lebanon's culture. People listen to music in shops, homes, and cars. One of Lebanon's most popular singers is Fairouz. During the **civil war**, she became a symbol of hope for the nation.

Lebanese people also enjoy sports. The most popular sports are soccer and basketball. People also like to ski in Lebanon's mountains. Swimming and **trekking** are popular, too.

Children enjoy a fun game of soccer in an open area near their homes.

Glossary

cabinet - a group of advisers chosen to lead government departments.

citrus - lemons, limes, oranges, grapefruits, or similar fruits.

civil war - a war between groups in the same country.

culture - the customs, arts, and tools of a nation or people at a certain time.

economy - the way a nation uses its money, goods, and natural resources.

fast - to go without food.

Hezbollah - a radical Shiite political party. Its guerrilla fighters were responsible for removing Israelis from southern Lebanon.

League of Nations - an international organization that promoted cooperation, peace, and security between nations. It functioned between 1920 and 1946.

minority - a racial, religious, or political group that is different from the larger group of which it is a part.

Muslim - a person who follows Islam. Islam is a religion based on the teachings of the prophet Muhammad as they appear in the Koran.

papyrus - a writing material made during ancient times.

prime minister - the highest-ranked member of some governments.

Ramadan - the ninth month of the Islamic year. Muslims do not eat from sunrise to sunset during this time period.

republic - a form of government in which authority rests with voting citizens and is carried out by elected officials, such as those in a parliament.

reserve - land set aside by the government for a specific purpose.

sect - a small group sharing the same beliefs and principles.

trek - a journey that involves difficulties or complex organization.

unique - being the only one of its kind.

Web Sites

To learn more about Lebanon, visit ABDO Publishing Company on the World Wide Web at **www.abdopub.com**. Web sites about Lebanon are featured on our Book Links page. These links are routinely monitored and updated to provide the most current information available.

Index